BIBLICAL. THEOLOGY FOR KIDS

MW01259607

TASTE & SEE

ALL ABOUT GOD'S GOODNESS

BY IRENE SUN

ILLUSTRATED BY HANNAH Y. LU

New Growth Press

New Growth Press, Greensboro, NC 27401
Text Copyright © 2022 by Irene Sun
Illustration Copyright © 2022 New Growth Press

Cover/Interior Design: Hannah Y. Lu
ISBN: 978-1-64507-235-5
Library of Congress Control Number: 2021952426
Printed in India

29 28 27 26 25 24 23 22   1 2 3 4 5

For my beloved and our boys, Emeth, Yohanan, Khesed, and Tobiah.

May we live and die for the Joy and the Table set before us.

"Come and have breakfast" (John 21:12).

–I. S.

To my husband, who eats far too quickly for anyone to share food

with him, but still chooses to save me some of every meal.

Of all the meals I have had, the best ones are with you.

And to the Giver of all good things, who in his love, gave us sushi.

– H. Y. L.

Sons and daughters, come and see,
How God's story came to be.

Darkness roamed over the deep,
Everything was fast asleep.

After darkness, there was light,
God made day, and God made night.

God brought food out of the ground,
All the world was safe and sound.

Mercy reigns from North to South,
Taste God's goodness in our mouth,

Grace abounds from West to East,
See God's table; it's a feast!

GENESIS 1:1–3

God made fruit trees green and bright,
Branches heavy, sweet delight.

Yellow lemon, berry blue,
Luscious apples grew and grew.

"Son and daughter, taste and see,
Find your happiness in me."

GENESIS 1:29–30

"I have only one decree,
Eat you must not from that tree."

Taste and see the Lord is good,
All our needs he understood.

Grace and mercy deep and wide,
Steadfast love is by your side.

GENESIS 2:16–17

Adam, Eve, deceived, misled,
They chose death and sinned instead.

They believed the serpent's lie,
God's Word did not satisfy.

Eve and Adam disobeyed,
They became ashamed, afraid.

Thorns and thistles, sin and pride,
Fears and pain, God's children died.

"Where's my daughter? Where's my son?
"What is this that you have done?"

When the sunlight went away,
Eve and Adam could not stay.

GENESIS 3

Pharaoh made God's people slaves,
Life was bitter. Who will save?

Baby Moses, in the reeds,
God provided every need.

Baby Moses, grew and grew,
Promises of God hold true.

EXODUS 1 AND 2

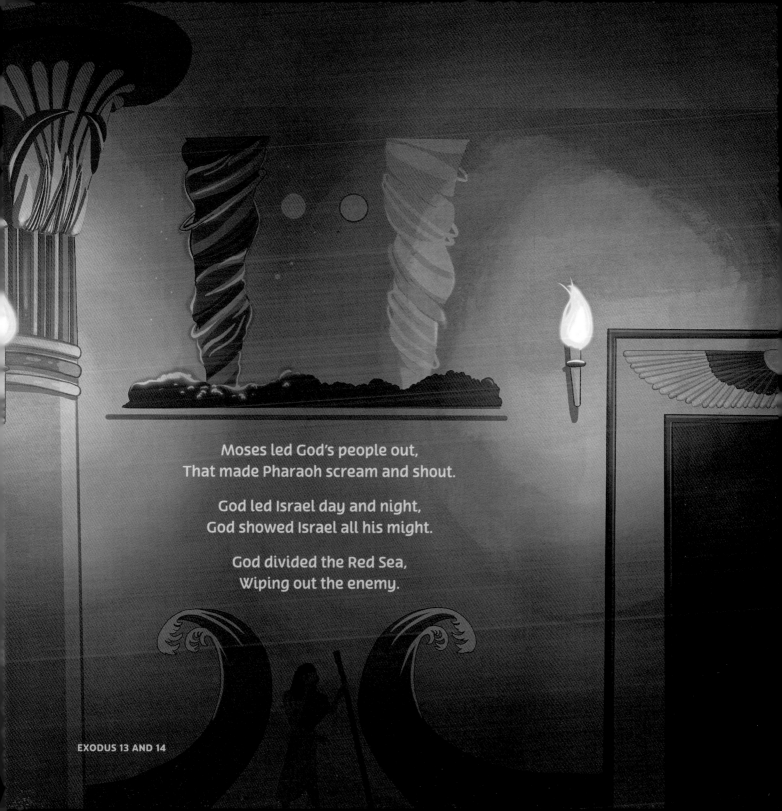

Moses led God's people out,
That made Pharaoh scream and shout.

God led Israel day and night,
God showed Israel all his might.

God divided the Red Sea,
Wiping out the enemy.

EXODUS 13 AND 14

Israel sang in gratitude,
Not for long—they wanted food!

Hungry people grumbled, groaned,
Thirsty people mumbled, moaned.

O how quickly they forgot
Pharaoh's folly, empty pots.

EXODUS 15
EXODUS 16:1–3

Do not worry, do not fret,
Father God will not forget.

Taste and see the Lord is good,
All our needs he understood.

Grace and truth will lead the way,
Steadfast love will always stay.

Warm and brilliant bread appears,
At first light for forty years.

Manna, manna from the sky,
Manna, manna satisfy.

Tasty, toasty, mercy seed,
Gather only what you need.

EXODUS 16:4–36

Taste and see his steadfast love,
Honey wafers from above.

Sons and daughters, can't you see?
God made you his family.

You were slaves but now you're free,
Sing the new song by the sea.

Long ago, at many times,
Prophets spoke and gave God's signs.

Jesus Christ, Immanuel,
God in flesh with us to dwell.

Thousands followed him around,
Teaching, healing, town to town.

HEBREWS 1:1–3
MATTHEW 1:23

Broken bodies, hungry eyes,
Growling stomachs, empty sighs.

Children eating Satan's lies,
Rotten fruit and muddy pies.

Dirty poison, things that choke,
Rocky rocks, and smoky smoke.

MATTHEW 14:13–14

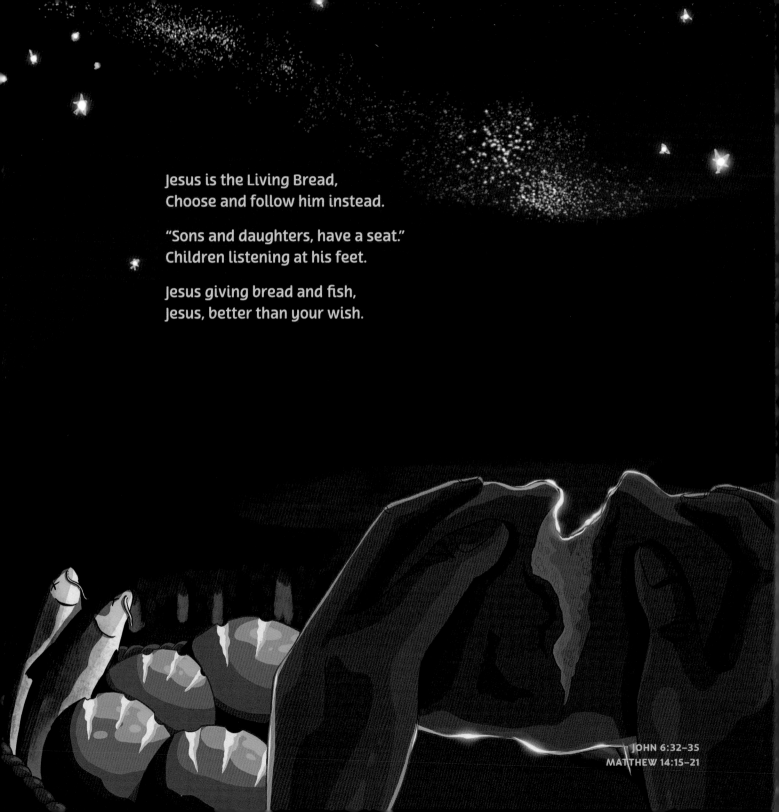

Jesus is the Living Bread,
Choose and follow him instead.

"Sons and daughters, have a seat."
Children listening at his feet.

Jesus giving bread and fish,
Jesus, better than your wish.

JOHN 6:32–35
MATTHEW 14:15–21

Jesus, light of truth and grace,
Eat with Jesus face to face.

Taste and see the Lord is good,
All our needs he understood.

Grace and mercy deep and wide,
Steadfast love is by your side.

JOHN 1:14

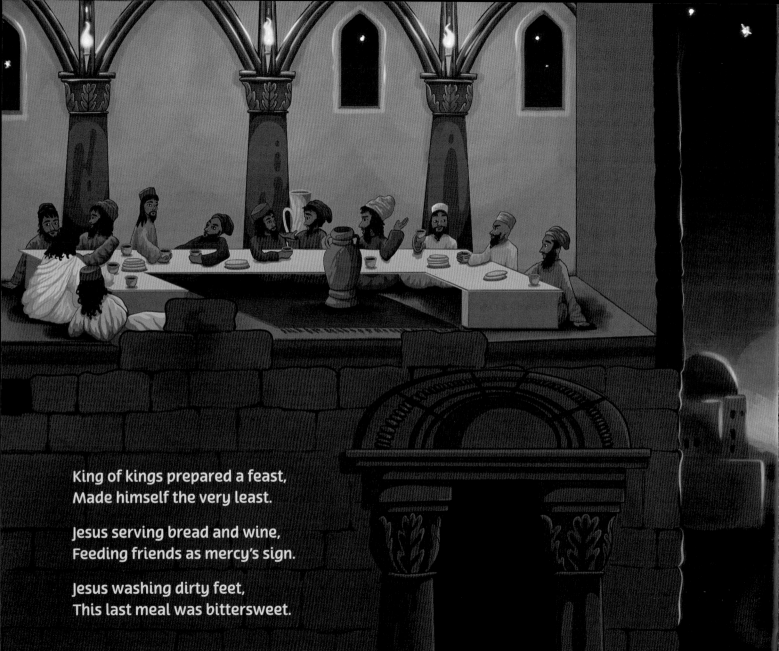

King of kings prepared a feast,
Made himself the very least.

Jesus serving bread and wine,
Feeding friends as mercy's sign.

Jesus washing dirty feet,
This last meal was bittersweet.

Twelve disciples in the light,
Soon, they'd stumble in the night.

Jesus praying on his knees,
All alone under the trees.

Jesus by his friends betrayed,
Danger came, they were afraid.

MARK 14:32–50

Jesus, him we crucified,
Jesus, for our sins he died.

Hands and feet nailed to the wood,
He gave us the Greatest Good.

On his head a crown of thorns,
Black and grey, ten thousand storms.

MARK 15:33–39

Taste and see the Lord is good,
All our needs he understood.

Grace and mercy deep and wide,
Steadfast love pierced on his side.

Broken bread and poured out wine,
I am his, and he is mine.

JOHN 19:33–35

Three days later, Jesus rose
From the grave with folded clothes.

Jesus went to Galilee,
Greeted brothers by the sea.

Brothers fished into the night,
After darkness, there was light.

"Children, children, come and eat."
Seven friends all took a seat.

Jesus served them fish and bread,
They remembered how they fled.

Grace and mercy, deep and vast,
"Do you love me?" Jesus asked.

JOHN 21:9–19

We are waiting for the feast,
Where the Lamb will be our peace.

At his table, we will sing,
In the presence of the King.

Marriage supper of the Lamb,
We will praise the great I AM.

Faith is sight and hope complete,
Love and righteousness will meet.

We will taste and we will see,
We will be one family.

King of heaven, we adore,
Feed us till we want no more.

REVELATION 19:6–10
PSALM 85:10

Holy Bible, good and true,
God speaks words to me and you.

Bread of heaven for our soul,
Milk and honey, make us whole.

Every morsel, every crumb,
Light the way till Jesus comes.

EZEKIEL 3:1–3
1 PETER 2:2
DEUTERONOMY 8:1–3

Taste and see the Lord is good,
All our needs he understood.

Truth and wisdom deep and vast,
God is first and God is last.

Sons and daughters, taste and see,
How God's story came to be.

Manna Cookies

Moses tells us that the people of Israel called the bread from heaven "manna," which means "what is it?" Manna was "white like coriander seed and tasted like wafers made with honey" (Exodus 16:31). Sesame seeds are a fair substitute for what manna might have looked like. This recipe turns sesame seeds into cookies that resemble wafers made with honey.

My sons call them "what-is-it cookies." You can also call them "Promised-Land cookies" because they contain milk (butter) and honey. The recipe can be made with either all-purpose or almond flour. If using almond flour, add an extra half cup of flour. This recipe makes a lot of wafer-thin cookies (40 to 45). Unlike the manna in the Bible, these cookies will not turn into worms the next day!

PREPARATION AND COOK TIME

1 hour (with a lot of help from children)

INGREDIENTS

¾ cup white sesame seeds

1¼ cups all-purpose flour OR 1¾ cups almond flour

¼ tsp baking powder

¾ cup salted butter (softened; add ½ tsp of salt if using unsalted butter)

1 cup sugar

¼ cup honey

1 tsp vanilla extract

2 large eggs

INSTRUCTIONS

1. Preheat oven to 350°F. Line two cookie sheets with parchment paper.

2. Toast sesame seeds in a pan over low heat for 5 minutes, until fragrant and golden brown.

3. Cream butter, sugar, vanilla extract, and honey together in a mixer for 5 minutes.

4. Add eggs one at a time until combined.

5. Fold in flour and baking powder.

6. Fold in sesame seeds.

7. On prepared baking sheets, place teaspoon-sized dollops of cookie dough 2–3 inches apart. These cookies will spread out, so be sure to leave plenty of room between dollops (approximately 12 cookies per baking sheet).

8. Bake for 10-12 minutes until golden brown rings appear around the cookies.

9. Let cookies cool for at least 5 minutes before removing from parchment paper.

10. Store cookies in layers separated with parchment paper to keep them from sticking together. Twice-bake the cookies (5 minutes in toaster oven and let cool) if you like them crunchy.

Teaching Your Child Biblical Theology

PREPARATION AND COOK TIME

A lifetime

INGREDIENTS

1 whole Bible, Old and New Testament

1 heaping spoonful of attentiveness and faithfulness

1 overflowing cup of awe and wonder

Immeasurable help from the Holy Spirit

Salt and light to taste (learning from pastors and teachers)

1. PREHEAT THE OVEN.

What is biblical theology?

Biblical theology helps us put together the Bible as one story. From "In the beginning" all the way to "Amen," the story of the Bible begins in Genesis and ends in Revelation. All the smaller stories of our creation, rebellion, redemption, and future hope have a place in the Great Story. Sixty-six books and over forty authors work together to tell the One Story of how God so loved the world and made himself known to us.

2. BRING THE INGREDIENTS TOGETHER.

What are some themes throughout Scripture?

Like all great stories, there are themes that run from the beginning to the end. The Bible has a few dozen major themes: king, priest, sacrifice, etc. This new series on biblical theology traces these themes for children to see how the smaller stories in the Bible are telling the One Great Story. Each book in this series follows each thread as they develop over the span of history.

Look, for example, at the Tree of Life. In Genesis, God placed the Tree of Life in the center of the garden of Eden. Whoever ate the fruit of this tree would live forever. When humanity rebelled against God, God cut them off from this tree (Genesis 2:9; 3:22–23). Having been cast out of the garden, the Bible revealed the way back: to "live by every word that comes from the mouth of the Lord" (Deuteronomy 8:3). Psalm 1 brings up the image of the tree, telling us that the person who meditates on God's Word day and night is like a tree, planted by streams of water (Psalm 1:2–3). In the New Testament, Jesus died on the cross—a tree—that we might have life (Galatians 3:13). The book of Revelation tells us about our hope for the dwelling place of God. It also tells us that the Tree of Life stands in the midst of the forever city, bearing twelve kinds of fruit (Revelation 22:2).

3. MIX WELL.
What is the purpose of biblical theology?

Biblical theology helps us see the wisdom of God, taste his goodness, stand in wonder, and bow in worship. God magnificently weaves these threads over the span of thousands of years to teach us about his faithfulness and steadfast love. Together, these threads come together to tell the One Great Story that gives life to all who will listen.

4. BAKE.
What is the purpose of tracing the theme of food in the Bible?

We trace the theme of food from Genesis to Revelation to see more clearly the goodness of God. In this world, food is often used as a reward for doing something good. In contrast, the Bible gives the picture of God feeding his people as an act of grace and mercy. He invites sinners and rebels to his table to show them his goodness.

Food declares the steadfast love and faithfulness of God. Food was the first gift God gave to his creatures (Genesis 1:29–30). Even after their rebellion, God provided food outside the garden. The Lord loves feeding his people when we least deserve his kindness. The Lord prepared a table for the Israelites in the wilderness when they complained and distrusted him (Exodus 16). Jesus fed the thousands who followed him for his gifts (John 6:1–51). He fed his disciples before and after they betrayed and denied him (John 13:26–38; 21:12).

5. SERVE.
How do we teach our children biblical theology about food?

The Lord has given us parents visible things to teach our children his invisible attributes. In eating and drinking the Lord's provision (visible), we taste and see his grace and mercy (invisible). At the communion table, we consume what is visible to remember our invisible God. The visible bread reminds us of Jesus giving his own body, and the visible cup reminds of his blood that was shed for the forgiveness of our sins.

We give thanks before meals, not only for the food set before us, but also for his grace and forgiveness.

We bake manna cookies (recipe in this book) to remember how God provides for our every need. I warm up cups of milk and honey for my toddler. Not only is his body nourished and comforted, but he is also drinking deeply the symbols and stories from Scripture. In Exodus, the Lord is leading his people to "a land flowing with milk and honey." Milk is a symbol for God's Word, and his Word is sweeter than honey (1 Peter 2:2; Psalm 19:10).

When we teach our children Biblical theology, "we're poor beggars telling other beggars where to find bread" (D. A. Carson).

6. ENJOY!
As you eat and drink, do so for his glory (1 Corinthians 10:31).

We magnify what we enjoy the most. We honor the worth, beauty, and goodness of what we love. When it comes to food, our enjoyment honors the maker of the good thing. When we enjoy grandma's cookies, we are honoring grandma and her love for us. In the same way, when we enjoy and savor the Word of God, we honor Christ who is the Word of God (John 1:1–3). To teach our children the Bible and theology is to say, "Taste and see that the Lord is good" (Psalm 34:8).